worship BAND PLAY-ALONG

KEYBOARD EDITION *Volume 4*

He Is Exalted

T0081540

Recorded and produced by Jim Reith at BeatHouse Music, Milwaukee, WI

Lead Vocals by Tonia Emrich and Jim Reith
Background Vocals by Jim Reith and Joy Palisoc Bach
Guitar by Jim Reith
Bass by Chris Kringel
Keyboard by Kurt Cowling
Drums by Del Bennett

ISBN 978-1-4234-1727-9

HAL•LEONARD® CORPORATION

7777 W. BLUEMOUND RD. P.O. BOX 13819 MILWAUKEE, WI 53213

Visit Hal Leonard Online at
www.halleonard.com

Beautiful One

Words and Music by Tim Hughes

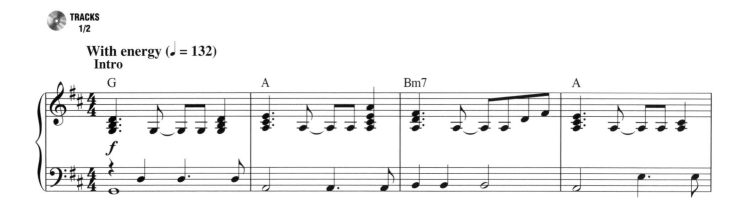

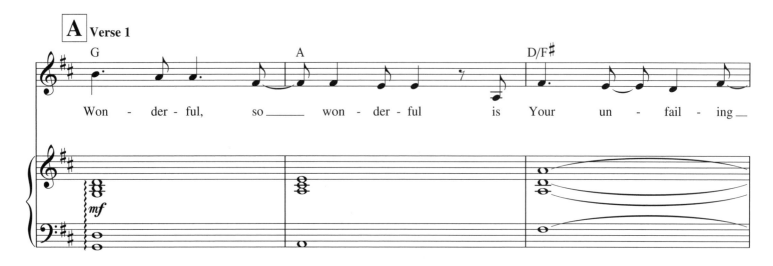

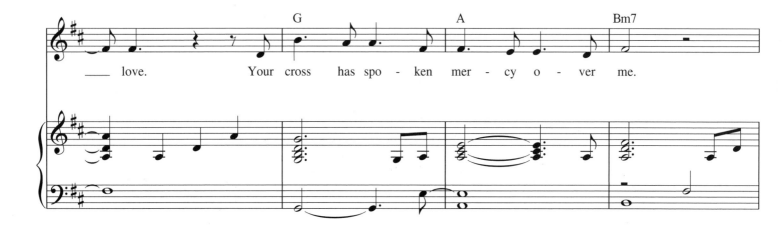

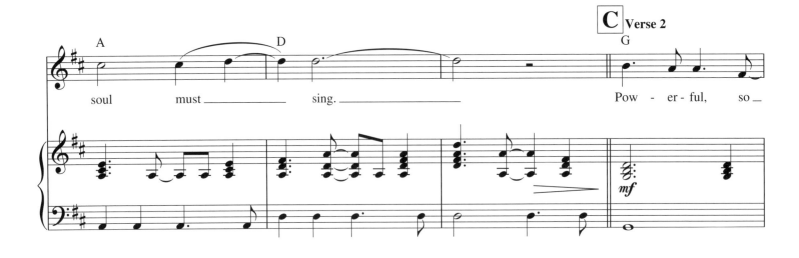

soul must _____ sing. _____ Pow - er - ful, so _____

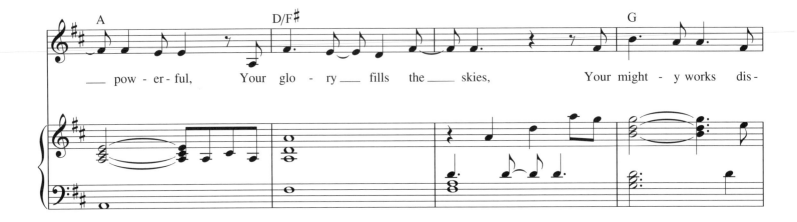

_____ pow - er - ful, Your glo - ry _____ fills the _____ skies, Your might - y works dis-

played for all to see. The beau - ty of Your _____

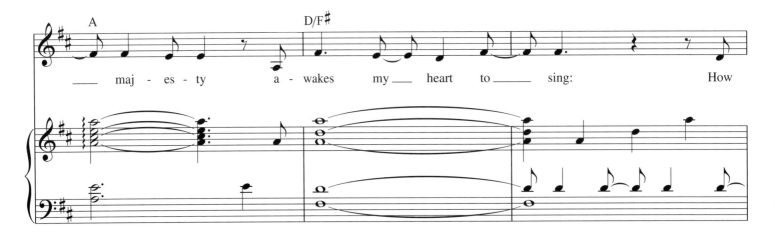

_____ maj - es - ty a - wakes my _____ heart to _____ sing: How

marvelous, how wonderful You are. _____ Beautiful

D Chorus

One I love, _____ Beautiful One I adore, Beautiful One, my soul must _____

dore, Beautiful One, my soul must _____

_____ sing. _____ Beautiful One I love, _____

Beau - ti - ful One I a - dore, Beau - ti - ful

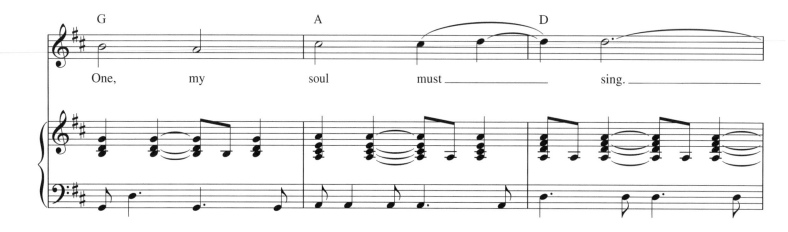

One, my soul must _____ sing. _____

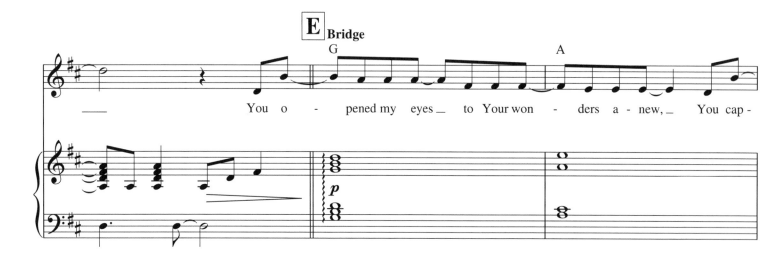

E **Bridge**

You o - pened my eyes ___ to Your won - ders a - new, ___ You cap -

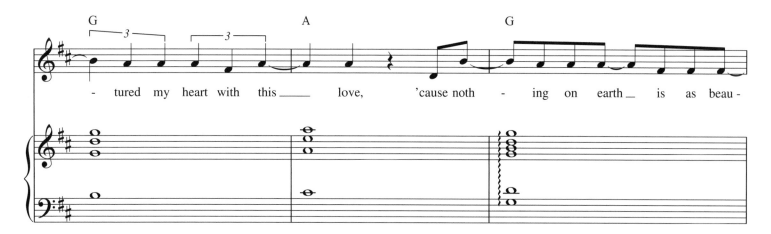

- tured my heart with this ___ love, 'cause noth - ing on earth ___ is as beau -

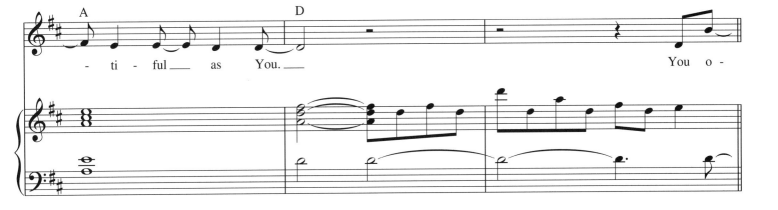

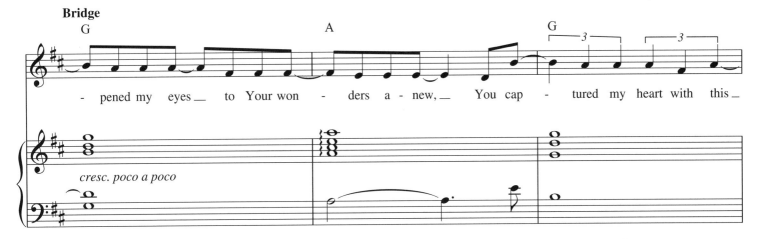

One I a - dore, Beau-ti-ful One, my

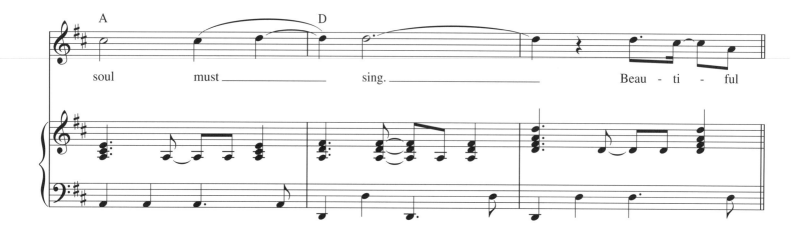

soul must _____ sing. _____ Beau-ti-ful

Chorus

One I love, ___ Beau-ti-ful One I a -

dore, Beau-ti-ful One, my soul must _____ sing.

God of All

Words and Music by Twila Paris

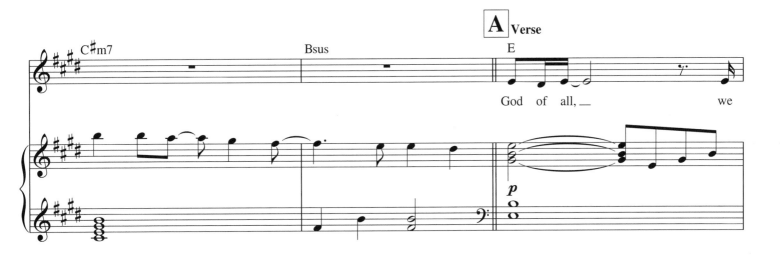

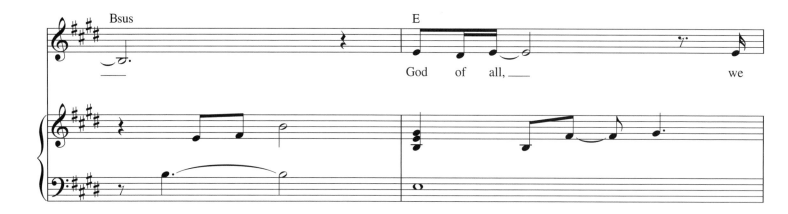

God of all, ___ we

come to praise ___ You. ___ We lift Your name ___ on high ___ in all ___ the earth. ___

B Chorus 1

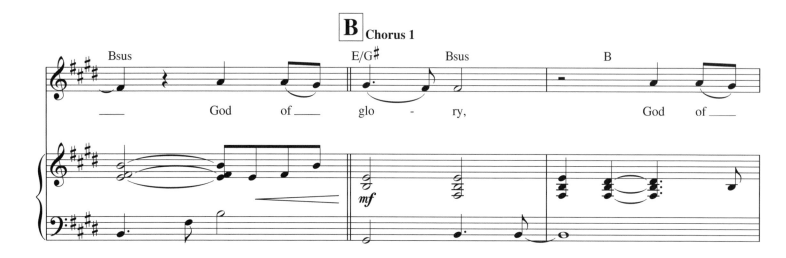

___ God of ___ glo - ry, God of ___

maj - es - ty, God of ___

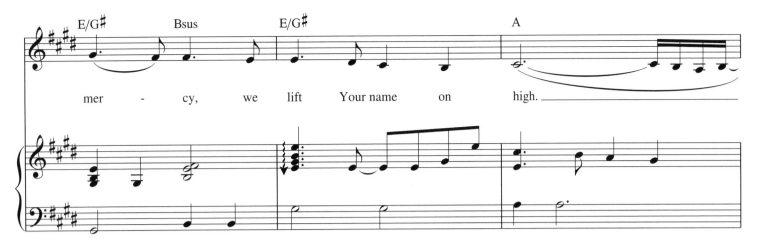

mer - cy, we lift Your name on high. _____

God of all, _____

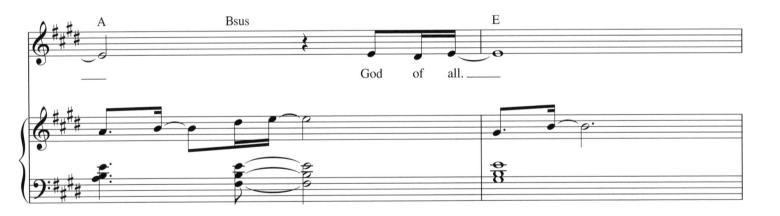

God of all. _____

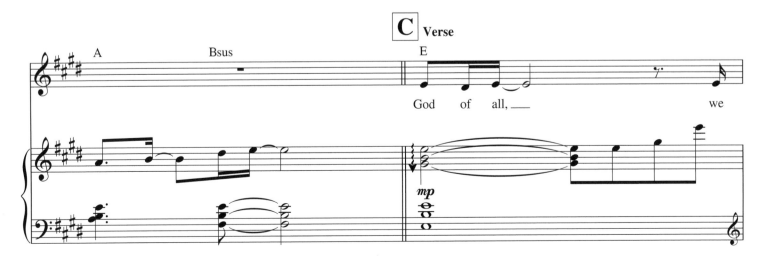

C Verse

God of all, _____ we

come to praise You. We lift Your name on high in all the earth.

God of all, we

come to praise You. We lift Your name on high in all the earth.

D **Chorus 2**

God of ho - li - ness,

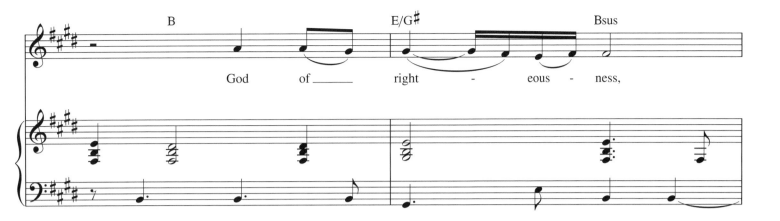

God of _____ right - eous - ness,

God of _____ heav - en, we lift Your name on

high. _____ God of ___ glo - ry,

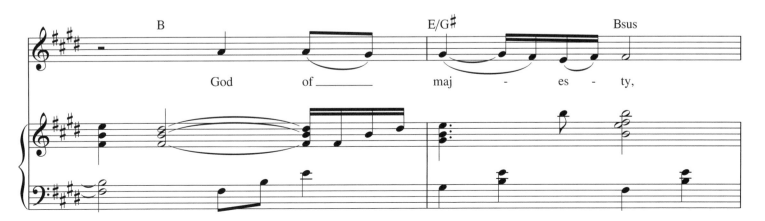

God of _____ maj - es - ty,

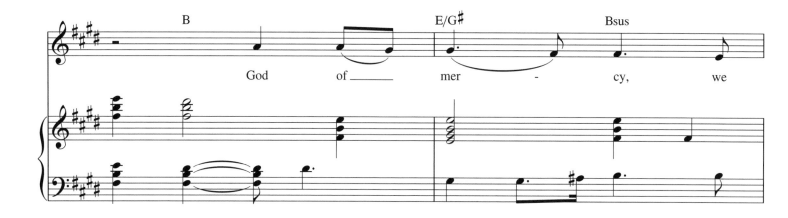

God of _____ mer - cy, we

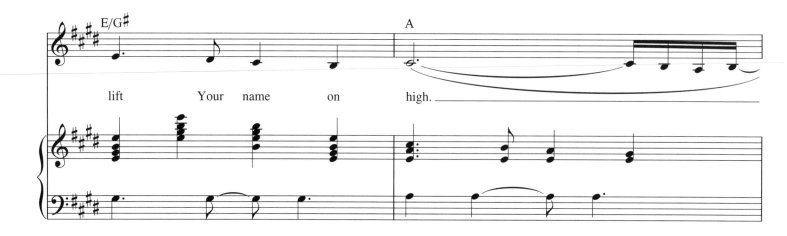

lift Your name on high. _____

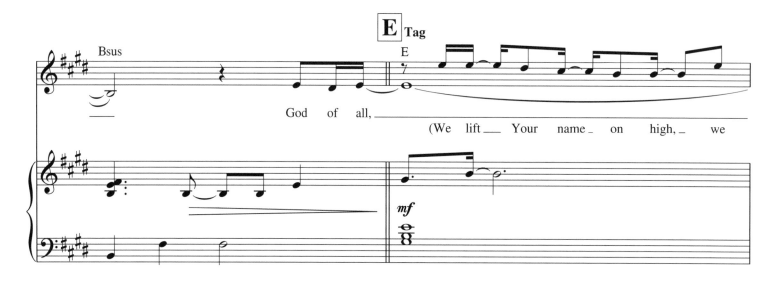

_____ God of all, _____

(We lift ___ Your name ___ on high, ___ we

E Tag

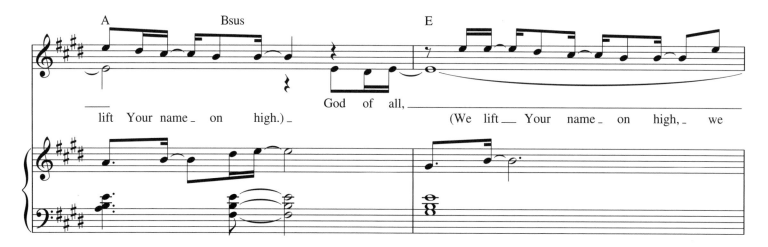

lift Your name ___ on high.) ___ God of all, _____

(We lift ___ Your name ___ on high, ___ we

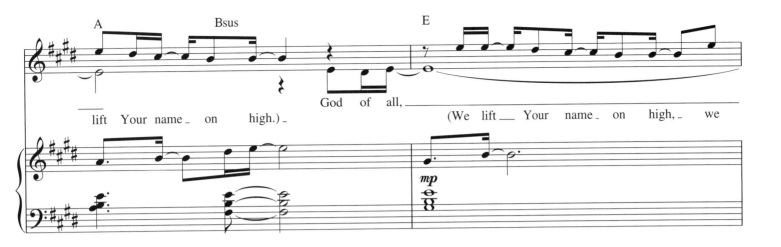

He Is Exalted

Words and Music by Twila Paris

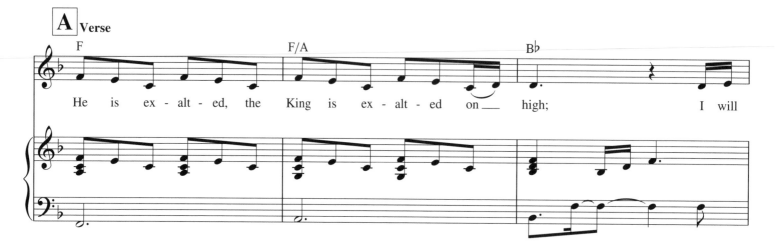

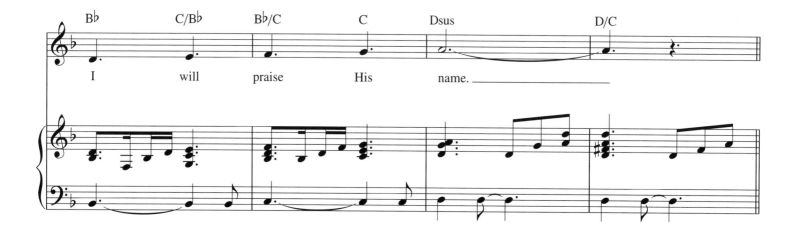

B Chorus

He is the Lord; for - ev - er His truth shall

reign. Heav - en and earth __ re -

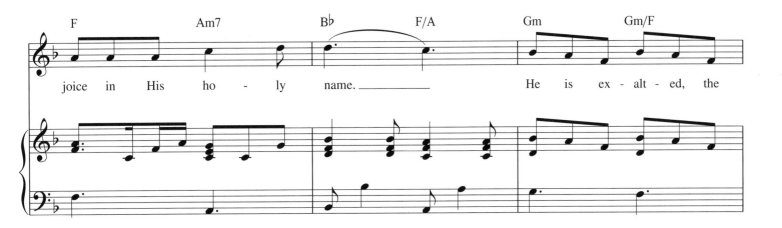

joice in His ho - ly name. _____ He is ex - alt - ed, the

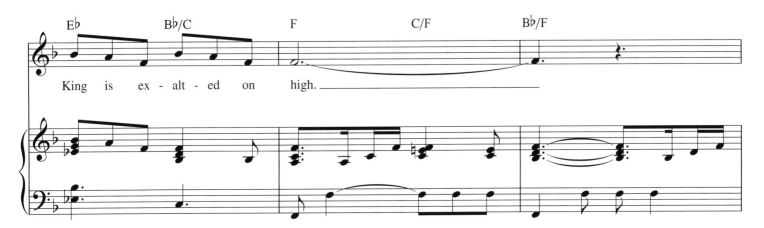

King is ex - alt - ed on high. _____

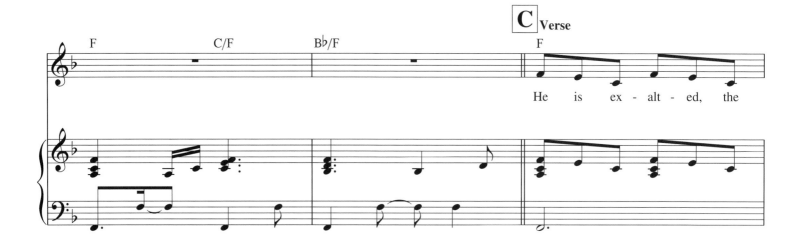

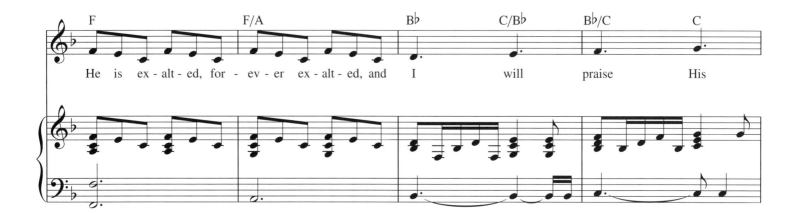

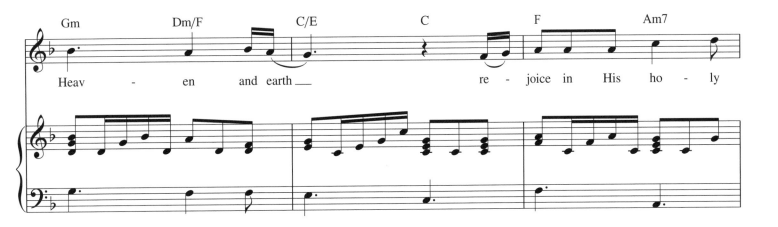

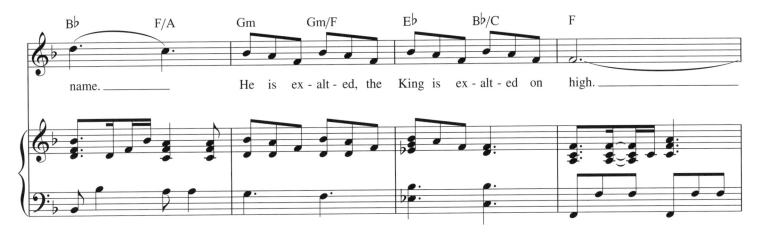

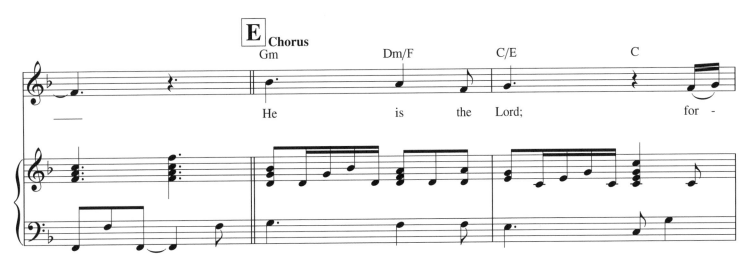

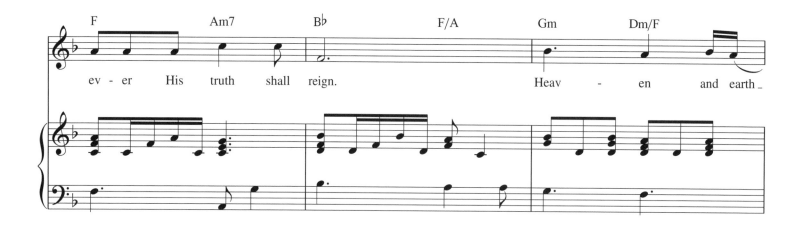

ev - er His truth shall reign. Heav - en and earth

re - joice in His ho - ly name.

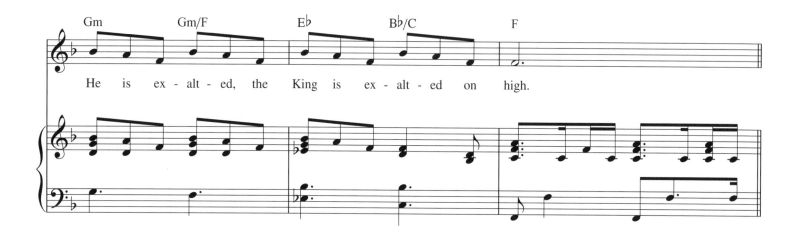

He is ex - alt - ed, the King is ex - alt - ed on high.

Tag

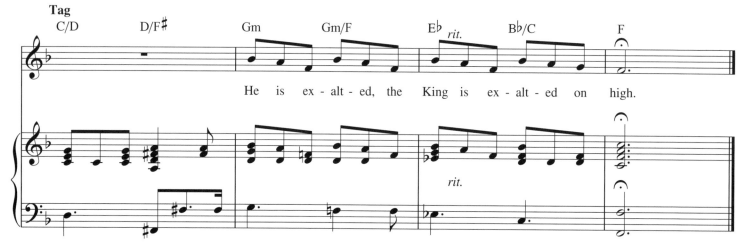

He is ex - alt - ed, the King is ex - alt - ed on high.

In Christ Alone

Words and Music by Keith Getty
and Stuart Townend

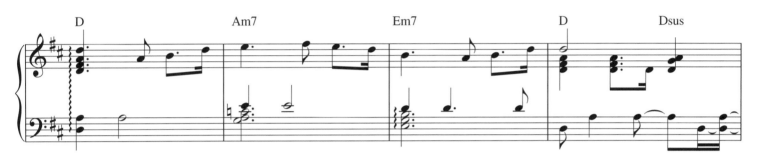

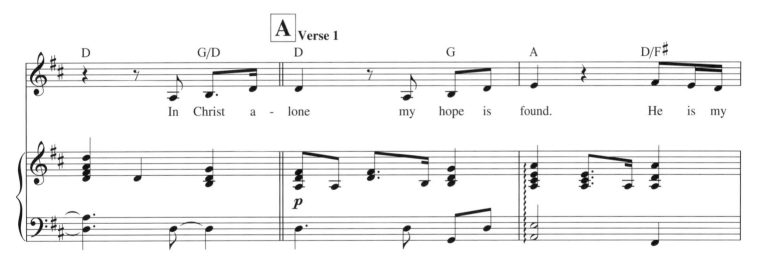

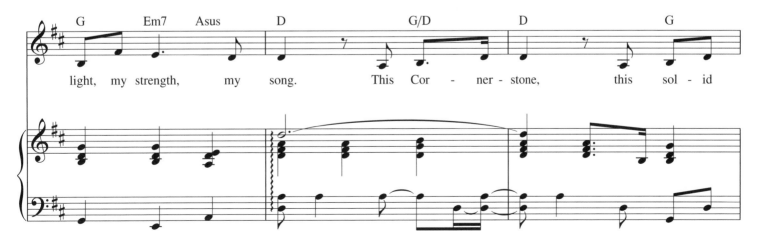

ground, firm through the fierc - est drought and storm. What heights of

love, what depths of peace, when fears are stilled, when striv - ings

cease. My Com - fort - er, my All in All, here in the

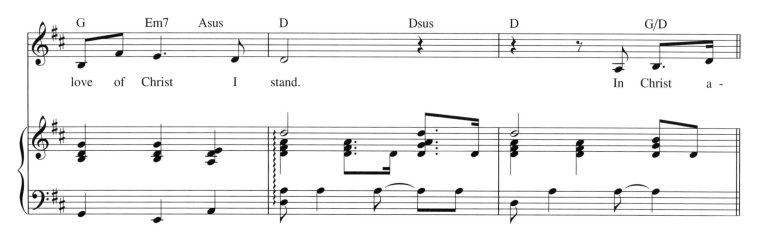

love of Christ I stand. In Christ a -

B Verse 2

lone, who took on flesh, full - ness of God in help - less

Babe. This gift of love and right-eous - ness, scorned by the

ones He came to save. 'Til on that cross as Je - sus

died, the wrath of God was sat - is - fied. For ev - 'ry

sin on Him was laid; here in the death of Christ I

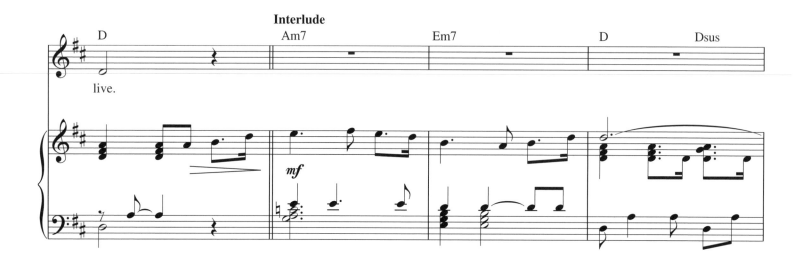

Interlude

live.

C Verse 3

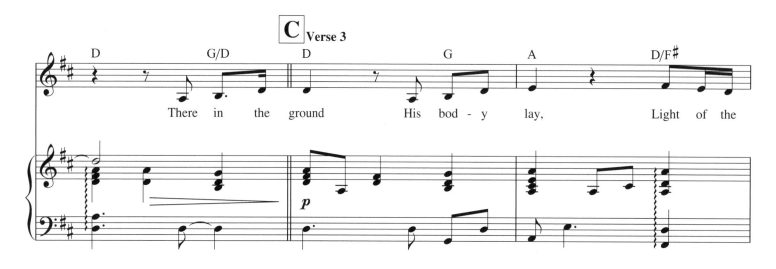

There in the ground His bod - y lay, Light of the

world by dark - ness slain. Then burst - ing forth in glo - rious

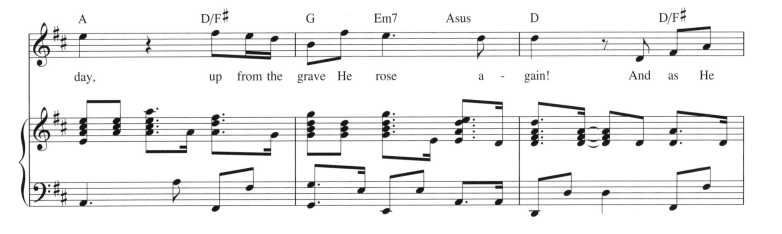

day,   up from the grave He rose a - gain! And as He

stands   in vic-to-ry,   sin's curse has lost   its grip on me.   For I am

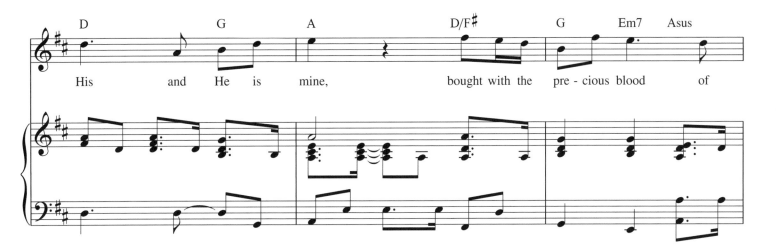

His   and He is mine,   bought with the pre-cious blood of

D Verse 4

Christ.   No guilt in life,   no fear in

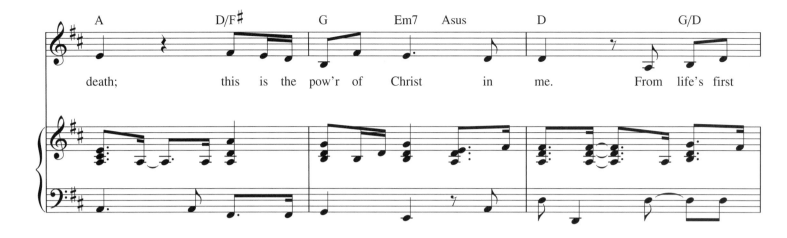

death; this is the pow'r of Christ in me. From life's first

cry to fi - nal breath, Je - sus com-mands my des - ti -

ny. No pow'r of hell, no scheme of man can ev - er

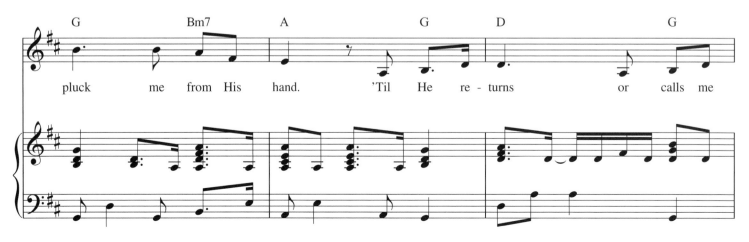

pluck me from His hand. 'Til He re - turns or calls me

Lord Most High

Words and Music by Don Harris and Gary Sadler

TRACKS
9/10

With motion (♩. = 54)

Intro

(verse A) **Verse**

From the ends of the earth, _ (From the ends of the earth,) _ from the

depths of the sea, _ (from the depths of the sea,) _ from the heights of the heav - ens, (from the

heights of the heav - ens, Your name be praised. Your name be praised.) From the

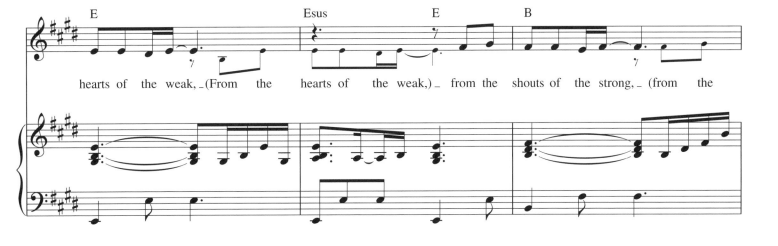

hearts of the weak, (From the hearts of the weak,) from the shouts of the strong, (from the

shouts of the strong,) from the lips of all peo - ple, (from the lips of all peo - ple, this

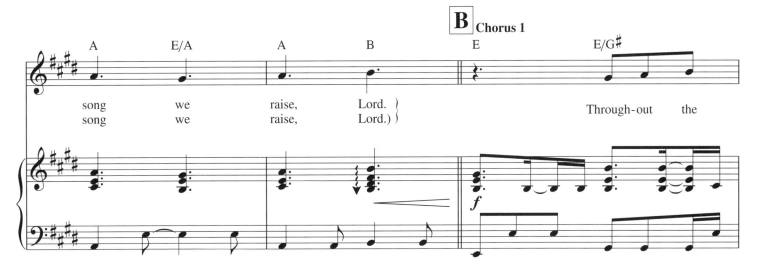

B Chorus 1

song   we   raise,   Lord. }
song   we   raise,   Lord.) }   Through-out the

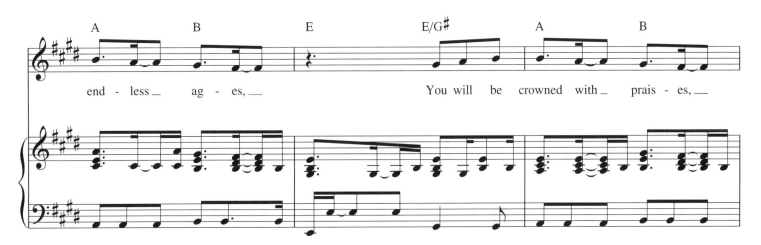

end - less   ag - es,   You will be crowned with   prais - es,

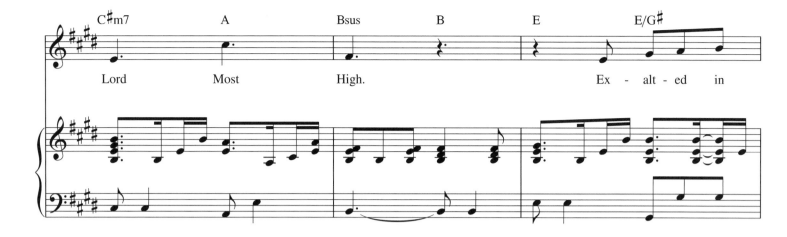

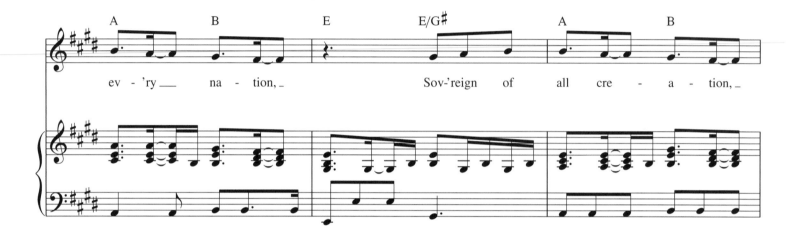

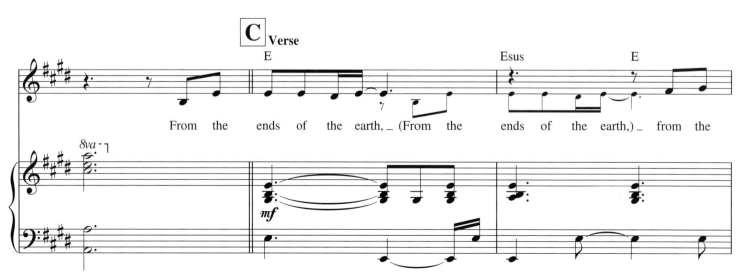

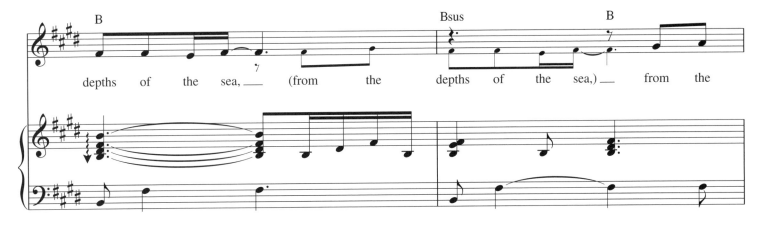

depths of the sea, ___ (from the depths of the sea,) ___ from the

heights of the heav - ens, Your name be
(from the heights of the heav - ens, Your name be

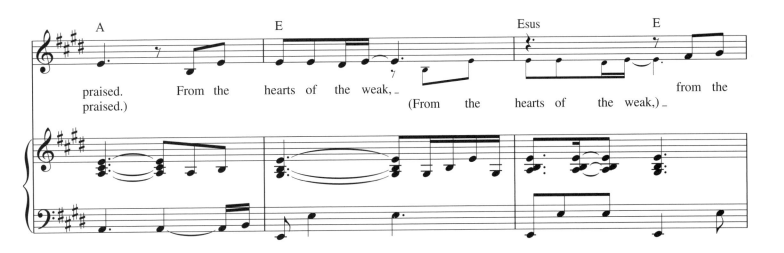

praised. From the hearts of the weak, ___ from the
praised.) (From the hearts of the weak,) ___

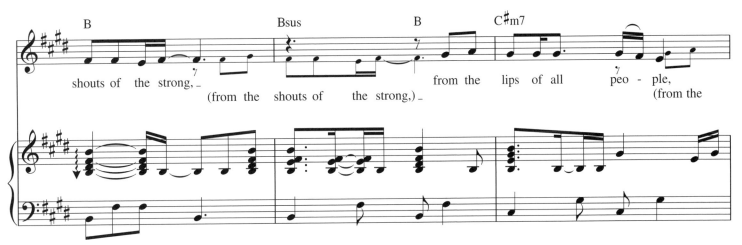

shouts of the strong, ___ from the lips of all peo - ple,
(from the shouts of the strong,) ___ (from the

this song we raise, Lord.
lips of all peo - ple, this song we raise, Lord,)

D Chorus 2

Through-out the end - less__ ag - es,__ You will be

crowned with_ prais - es,__ Lord Most High.

Ex - alt - ed in ev - 'ry__ na - tion,__ Sov -'reign of

all cre - a - tion,___ Lord Most High.

E Chorus 1

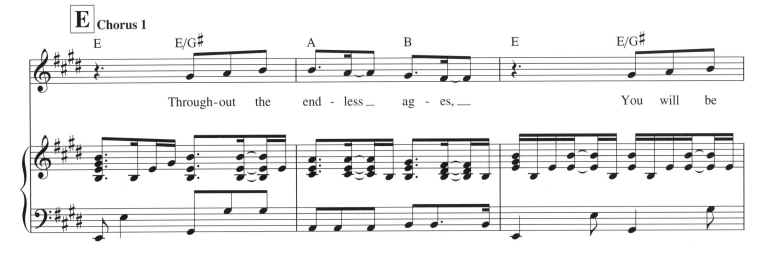

Through-out the end - less___ ag - es,___ You will be

crowned with___ prais - es,___ Lord Most High.

Ex - alt - ed in ev - 'ry___ na - tion,___ Sov-'reign of

all cre - a - tion, _ Lord Most High, be mag - ni - fied. _

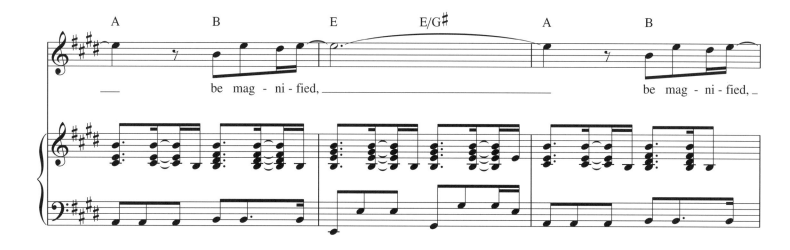

Be mag - ni - fied, ____

be mag - ni - fied, ____ be mag - ni - fied, _

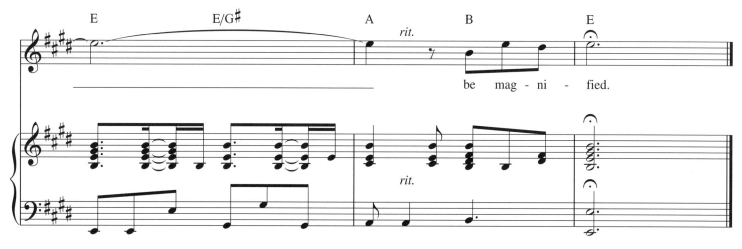

be mag - ni - fied.

Lord, Reign in Me

Words and Music by Brenton Brown

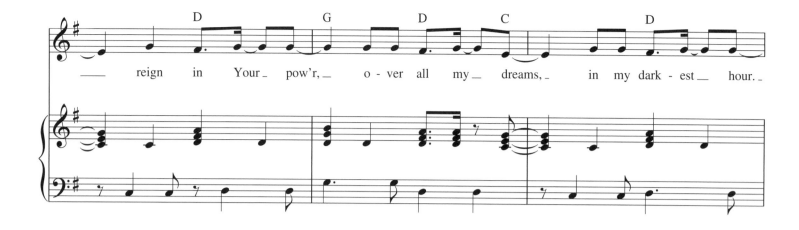

reign in Your pow'r, o - ver all my dreams, in my dark - est hour.

You are the Lord of all I am, so won't You

Interlude

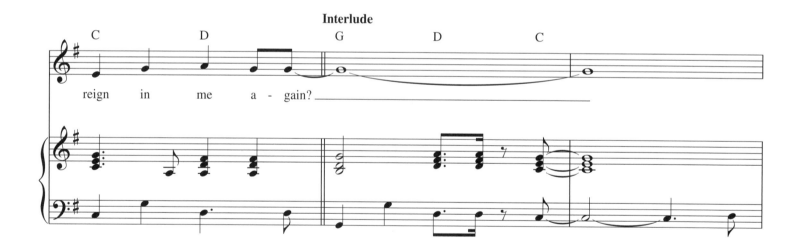

reign in me a - gain? _____

C | **Verse 2**

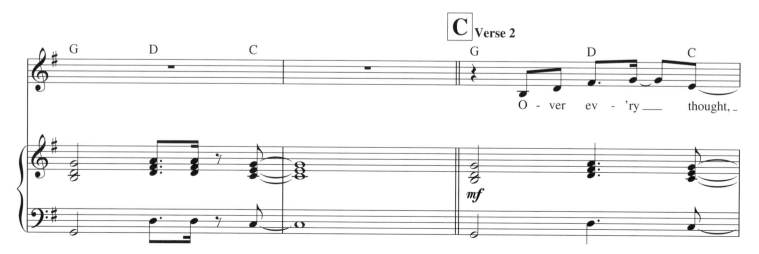

O - ver ev - 'ry thought,

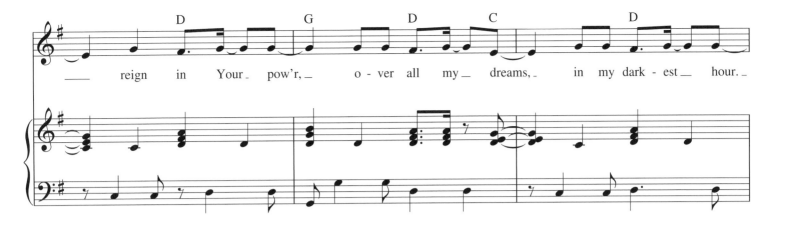

reign in Your pow'r, o - ver all my dreams, in my dark - est hour.

You are the Lord of all I am, so won't You

reign in me a - gain? Won't You reign in me a - gain?

Outro

We Want to See Jesus Lifted High

Words and Music by Doug Horley

We want to see Je - sus lift - ed high, ___ a ban - ner that flies _

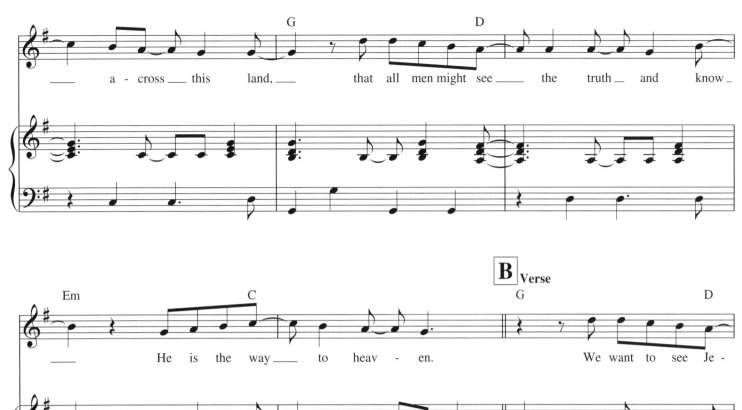

a - cross _ this land, _ that all men might see _ the truth _ and know _

B Verse

_ He is the way _ to heav - en. We want to see Je -

- sus lift - ed high, _ a ban - ner that flies _ a - cross _ this land, _

_ that all men might see _ the truth _ and know _ He is the way _

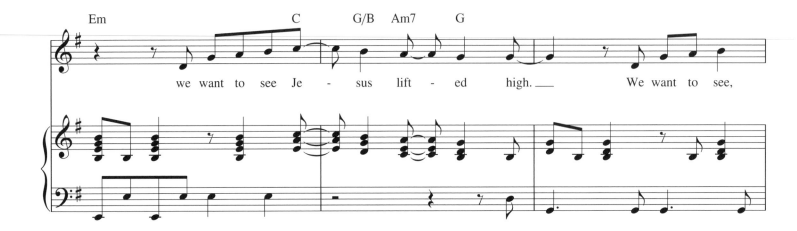

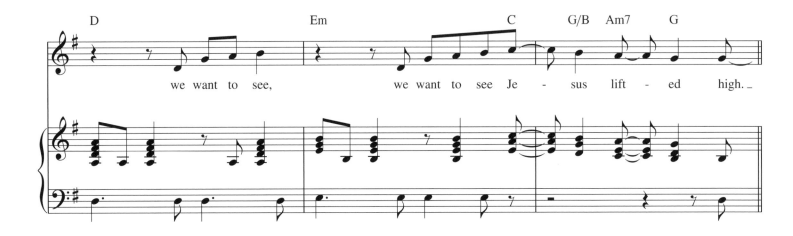

come tum-bl-ing down ___ and down ___ and down ___ and down. ___

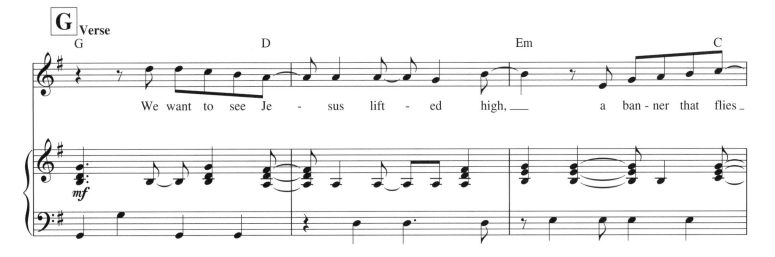

G **Verse**

We want to see Je-sus lift-ed high, ___ a ban-ner that flies ___

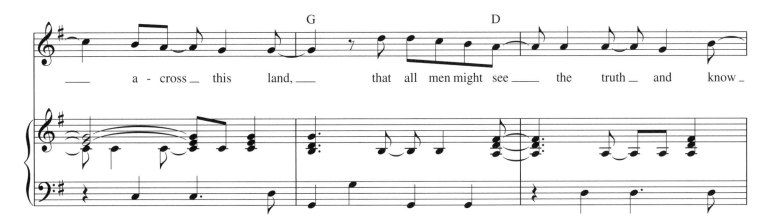

___ a-cross __ this land, ___ that all men might see ___ the truth __ and know __

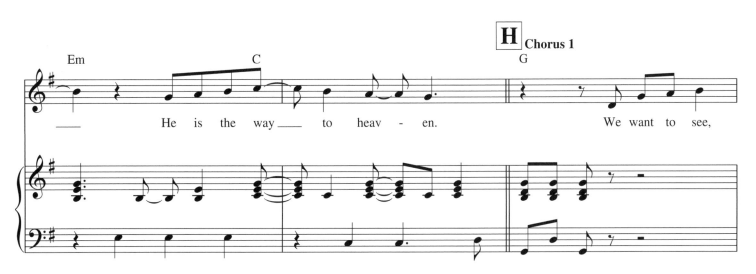

H **Chorus 1**

___ He is the way ___ to heav - en. We want to see,

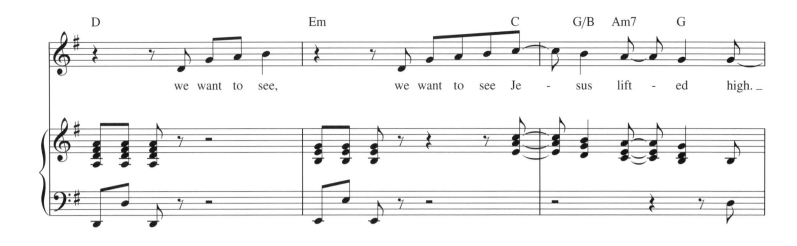

we want to see, we want to see Je - sus lift - ed high. _

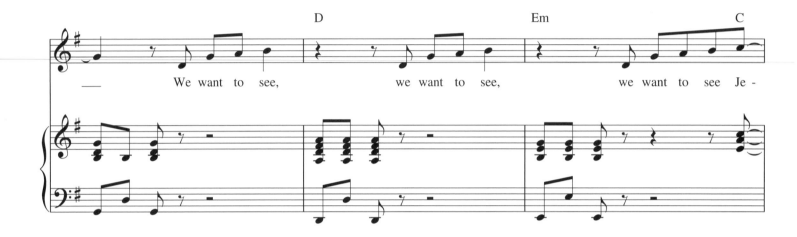

_ We want to see, we want to see, we want to see Je -

I **Chorus 2**

- sus lift - ed high. ____ We're gon - na see, we're gon - na see,

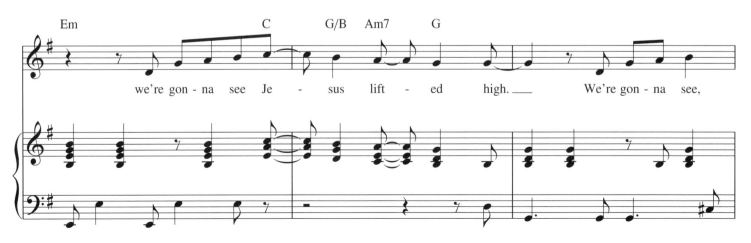

we're gon - na see Je - sus lift - ed high. ____ We're gon - na see,

we're gon - na see, we're gon - na see Je - sus lift - ed high.

J **Outro**

We're gon - na see Je -

- sus lift - ed high.

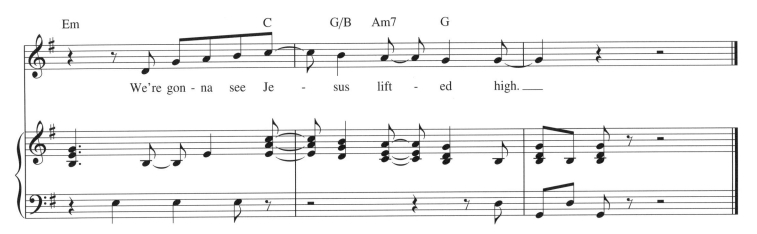

We're gon - na see Je - sus lift - ed high.

Worthy Is the Lamb

Words and Music by Darlene Zschech

love, Lord. _____ Thank You for the nail - pierced hands._

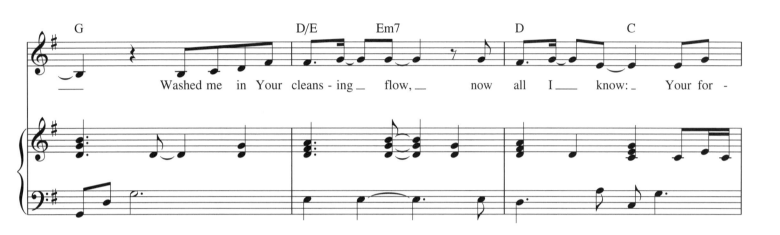

_____ Washed me in Your cleans - ing _ flow, _ now all I _ know: _ Your for -

B Chorus

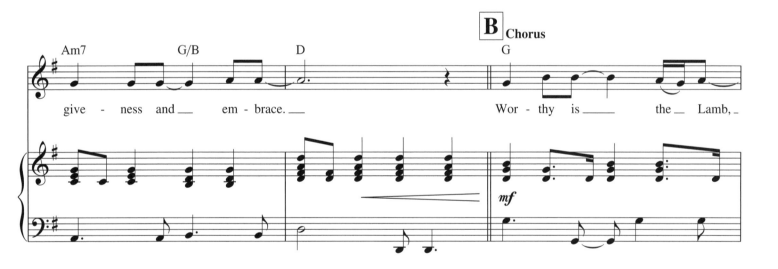

give - ness and _ em - brace. _ Wor - thy is _____ the _ Lamb, _

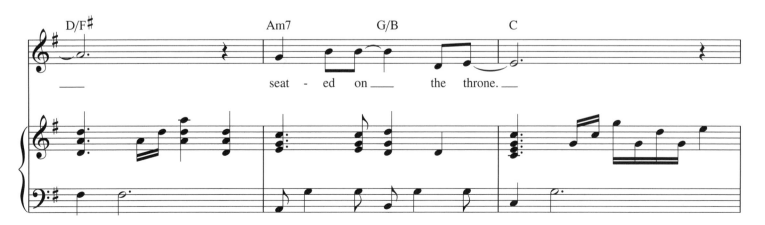

seat - ed on _____ the throne. _

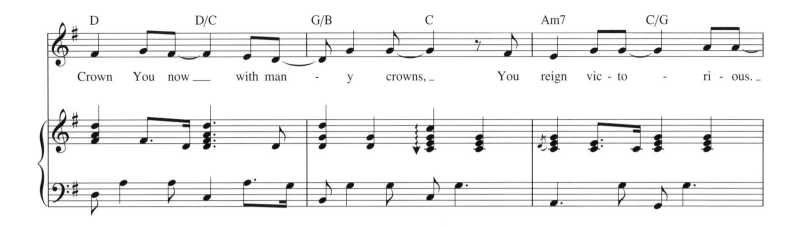

Crown You now __ with man - y crowns, __ You reign vic - to - ri - ous. __

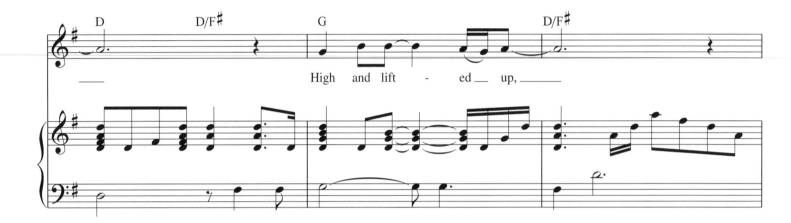

__ High and lift - ed __ up, __

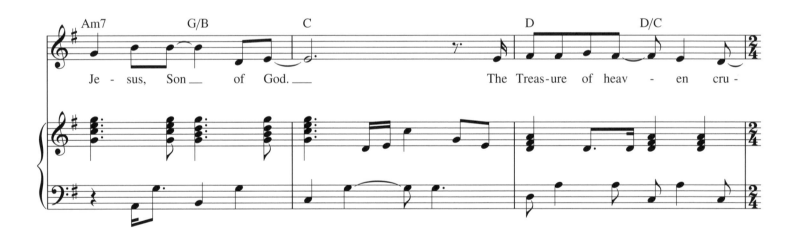

Je - sus, Son __ of God. __ The Treas-ure of heav - en cru -

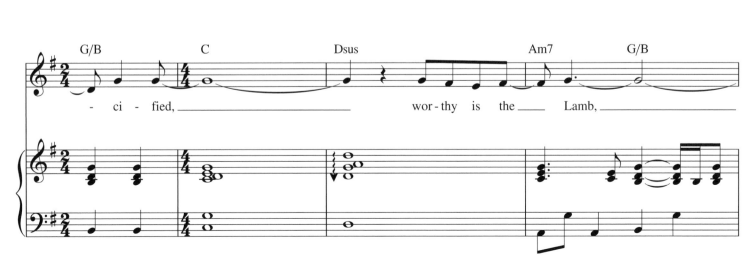

- ci - fied, __ wor-thy is the __ Lamb, __

worthy is the Lamb. Thank You for the

C Verse

cross, Lord. Thank You for the price You paid.

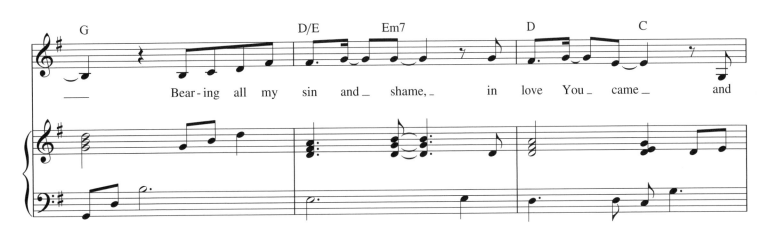

Bearing all my sin and shame, in love You came and

gave amazing grace. Thank You for this love, Lord.

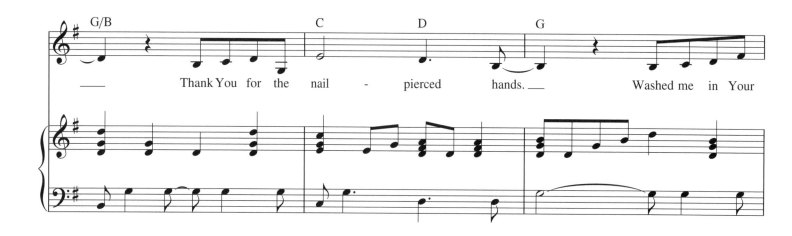

Thank You for the nail - pierced hands. __ Washed me in Your

cleans - ing __ flow, __ now all I __ know: __ Your for - give - ness and __ em - brace. __

D Chorus

Wor - thy is __ the __ Lamb, __

seat - ed on __ the throne. __ Crown You now __ with man -

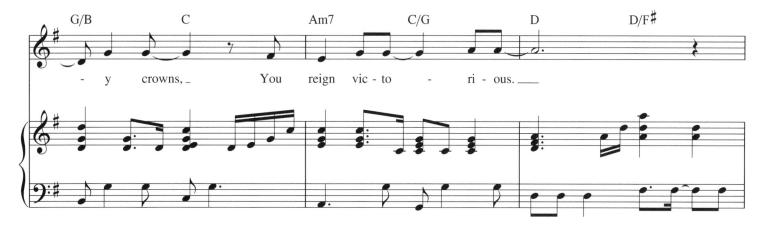

- y crowns, __ You reign vic - to - ri - ous. __

High and lift - ed __ up, _____ Je - sus, Son __ of God. __

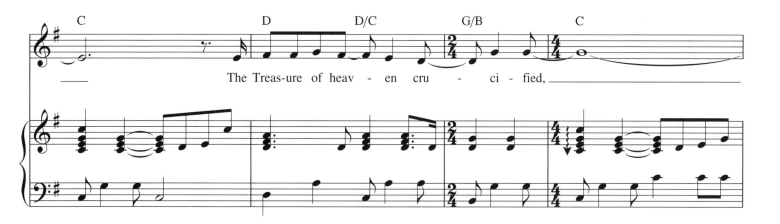

___ The Treas-ure of heav - en cru - ci - fied, _____

___ wor - thy is the __ Lamb, _____ wor - thy is the __

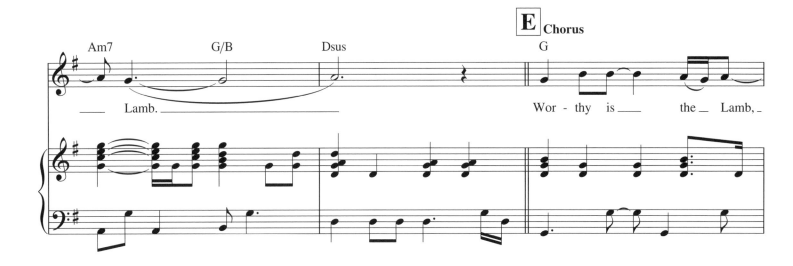

Lamb. Wor - thy is ___ the ___ Lamb, ___

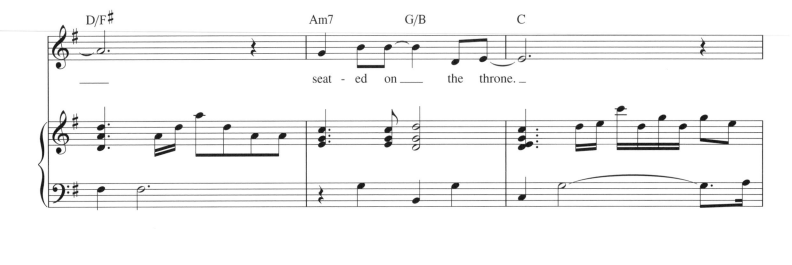

seat - ed on ___ the throne. ___

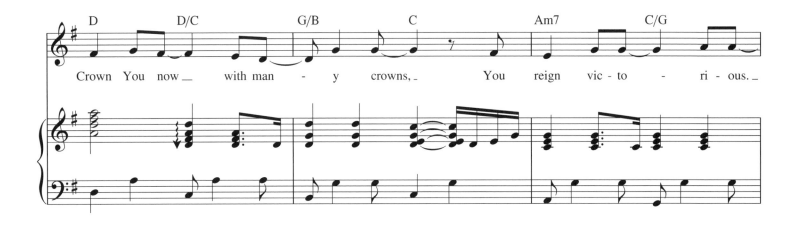

Crown You now ___ with man - y crowns, ___ You reign vic - to - ri - ous. ___

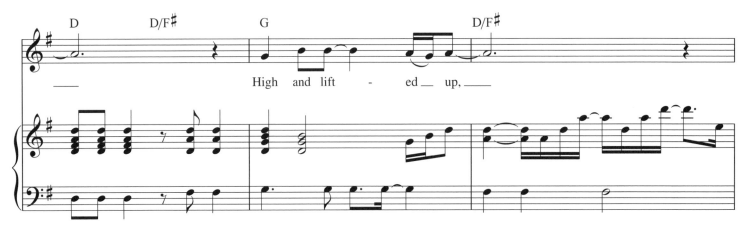

High and lift - ed ___ up, ___

Je - sus, Son of God. The Treas-ure of heav - en cru -

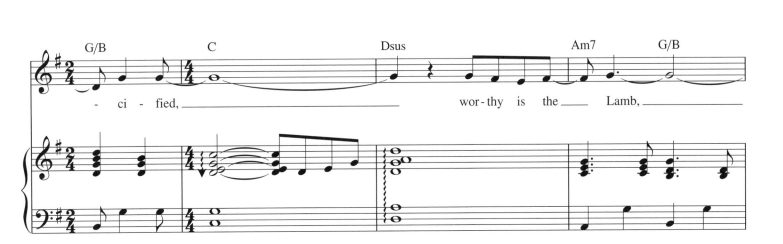

- ci - fied, wor-thy is the Lamb,

F **Tag**

wor-thy is the Lamb. Wor-thy is the Lamb,

wor-thy is the Lamb. Wor-thy is the Lamb.

BEAUTIFUL ONE

TIM HUGHES

Key of **D Major**, 4/4

INTRO:

G A Bm7 A

G A D

VERSE 1:

G　　　　A　　　D/F♯
Wonderful, so wonderful is Your unfailing love

　　　G　　　　A　　　Bm7
Your cross has spoken mercy over me

　　G　　　　A　　　　D/F♯
No eye has seen, no ear has heard, no heart could fully know

　　G　　　　A　　　D
How glorious, how beautiful You are

CHORUS:

　　　　G　　A　　　G　　A
Beautiful One I love, Beautiful One I adore

　　　G　　A　　　D
Beautiful One, my soul must sing

VERSE 2:

G　　　　A　　　D/F♯
Powerful, so powerful, Your glory fills the skies

　　G　　　　A　　　Bm7
Your mighty works displayed for all to see

　　G　　　　A　　　D/F♯
The beauty of Your majesty awakes my heart to sing:

　　G　　　　A　　　D
How marvelous, how wonderful You are

(REPEAT CHORUS 2X)

BRIDGE (2X):

　　G　　　　　　　　A
You opened my eyes to Your wonders anew

　　G　　　　　　　A
You captured my heart with this love

　　　G　　　　　　A　　　D
'Cause nothing on earth is as beautiful as You

(REPEAT CHORUS 2X)

GOD OF ALL
TWILA PARIS

Key of **E Major, 4/4**

INTRO (2X):

E   B/D♯   C♯m7   Bsus

VERSE:

E   B/D♯
God of all, we come to praise You

  A/C♯   Bsus
We lift Your name on high in all the earth

E   B/D♯
God of all, we come to praise You

  A/C♯   Bsus
We lift Your name on high in all the earth

CHORUS 1:

     E/G♯ Bsus   B   E/G♯   Bsus   B
God of glo - ry,   God of maj - es - ty

     E/G♯ Bsus E/G♯   A   Bsus
God of mer - cy, we lift Your name on high

     E A Bsus   E A Bsus
God of all,   God of all

(REPEAT VERSE)

CHORUS 2:

    E/G♯   Bsus   B   E/G♯   Bsus   B
God of ho - li - ness,   God of righteousness

    E/G♯   Bsus E/G♯   A   Bsus
God of heav - en, we lift Your name on high

  E/G♯ Bsus   B   E/G♯   Bsus   B
God of glo - ry,   God of maj - es - ty

    E/G♯ Bsus E/G♯   A   Bsus
God of mer - cy, we lift Your name on high

TAG:

    E   A   Bsus
God of all (We lift Your name on high, we lift Your name on high) **REPEAT 4X**

    E (hold)
God of all

HE IS EXALTED

TWILA PARIS

Key of **F Major, 6/8**

INTRO:

F C/F B♭/F

F C/F B♭/F

VERSE:

F   F/A   B♭
He is exalted, the King is exalted on high

      B♭/D   C/E
I will praise Him

F   F/A
He is exalted, forever exalted

     B♭   C/B♭   B♭/C   C   Dsus   D/C
And I   will   praise His name

CHORUS:

Gm Dm/F   C/E   C
He   is the Lord

      F   Am7   B♭   F/A
Forever His truth shall reign

Gm Dm/F   C/E   C
Heav - en and earth

      F   Am7 B♭   F/A
Rejoice in His holy name

Gm   Gm/F   E♭   B♭/C   (F)
He is exalted, the King is exalted on high

(REPEAT INTRO)

(REPEAT VERSE)

(REPEAT CHORUS 2X)

TAG:

C/D D/F♯ Gm   Gm/F   E♭   B♭/C   F (hold)
            He is exalted, the King is exalted on high

IN CHRIST ALONE

KEITH GETTY and STUART TOWNEND

Key of **D Major**, 3/4

INTRO (2X):

Am7   **Em7**   **D Dsus D**

VERSE 1:

G/D   D   G   A
In Christ alone my hope is found

D/F♯   G   Em7 Asus   D
He is my light, my strength,   my song

G/D   D   G   A
This Cornerstone, this solid ground

D/F♯   G   Em7 Asus   D
Firm through the fiercest drought and storm

D/F♯   G   D/F♯   A
What heights of love, what depths of peace

D/F♯   G   Bm7   A
When fears are stilled when strivings cease

G   D   G   A
My Comforter, my All in All

D/F♯   G   Em7 Asus D
Here in the love of Christ   I stand

(Dsus D)

VERSE 2:

In Christ alone, who took on flesh
Fullness of God in helpless Babe
This gift of love and righteousness
Scorned by the ones He came to save
'Til on that cross as Jesus died
The wrath of God was satisfied
For ev'ry sin on Him was laid
Here in the death of Christ I live

INTERLUDE:

Am7   **Em7**   **D Dsus D**

VERSE 3:

There in the ground His body lay
Light of the world by darkness slain
Then bursting forth in glorious day
Up from the grave He rose again!
And as He stands in victory
Sin's curse has lost its grip on me
For I am His and He is mine
Bought with the precious blood of Christ

(Dsus D)

VERSE 4:

No guilt in life, no fear in death
This is the pow'r of Christ in me
From life's first cry to final breath
Jesus commands my destiny
No pow'r of hell, no scheme of man
Can ever pluck me from His hand
'Til He returns or calls me home
Here in the pow'r of Christ I'll stand

TAG:

D/F♯   G   D/F♯   A
No pow'r of hell, no scheme of man

D/F♯ G   Bm7   A
Can ever pluck me from His hand

G   D   G   A
'Til He returns or calls me home

D/F♯   G   Em7 Asus   D
Here in the pow'r of Christ   I'll stand

D/F♯   G   Em7 Asus   D (hold)
Here in the pow'r of Christ   I'll stand

LORD MOST HIGH

DON HARRIS and GARY SADLER

TRACKS 9/10

Key of **E Major**, **6/8**

INTRO (2X):

E   Esus   E   Esus2

VERSE:

          E   *Echo:* Esus   E
From the ends of the earth (from the ends of the earth)
          B   Bsus   B
From the depths of the sea (from the depths of the sea)
        C♯m7
From the heights of the heavens (from the heights of the heavens)
     A E/A A
Your name be praised
          E   Esus   E
From the hearts of the weak (from the hearts of the weak)
          B   Bsus   B
From the shouts of the strong (from the shouts of the strong)
        C♯m7
From the lips of all people (from the lips of all people)
     A E/A A   B
This song we raise, Lord

CHORUS 1:

E E/G♯   A   B
Throughout the endless ages
E E/G♯   A   B
You will be crowned with praises
C♯m7 A Bsus B
Lord Most High
E E/G♯   A   B
Exalted in ev'ry nation
E E/G♯   A   B
Sov'reign of all creation
C♯m7 A   B E/G♯   A
Lord Most High, be magnified

(REPEAT VERSE)

CHORUS 2:

E E/G♯   A   B
Throughout the endless ages
E E/G♯   A   B
You will be crowned with praises
C♯m7 A Bsus B
Lord Most High
E   E/G♯   A   B
Exalted in ev'ry nation
E E/G♯   A   B
Sov'reign of all creation
C♯m7 A Bsus B
Lord Most High

(REPEAT CHORUS 1)

TAG:

B   E E/G♯ A
      Be magnified   **REPEAT 2X**
B   E (hold)
Be magnified

LORD, REIGN IN ME

BRENTON BROWN

TRACKS
11/12

Key of **G Major, 4/4**

INTRO:

G D C   G D C

VERSE 1:

G   D   C   D
    Over all the earth, You reign on high

G   D   C   D
    Ev'ry mountain stream, ev'ry sunset sky

Em7   D   C   D Am7
    But my one request, Lord, my only aim

           C   D
Is that You'd reign in me again

CHORUS:

G   D   C   D
    Lord, reign in me, reign in Your pow'r

G   D   C   D
    Over all my dreams, in my darkest hour

Em7   D   C   D Am7
    You are the Lord of all I am

           C   D
So won't You reign in me again?

INTERLUDE:

G D C   G D C

VERSE 2:

G   D   C   D
    Over ev'ry thought, over ev'ry word

G   D   C   D
    May my life reflect the beauty of my Lord

Em7   D   C   D Am7
    'Cause You mean more to me than any earthly thing

           C   D
So won't You reign in me again?

(REPEAT CHORUS 3X)

TAG:

Am7   C   D
    Won't You reign in me again?

OUTRO:

G D C   G D C (hold)

WE WANT TO SEE JESUS LIFTED HIGH

DOUG HORLEY

Key of **G Major**, 4/4

INTRO (2X):

G D   Em C

VERSE:

G   D
   We want to see Jesus lifted high
Em   C
   A banner that flies across this land
G   D
   That all men might see the truth and know
Em   C
   He is the way to heaven

(REPEAT VERSE)

CHORUS 1:

G   D
   We want to see,   we want to see
Em   C G/B Am7 G
   We want to see Je - sus   lift - ed high
G   D
   We want to see,   we want to see
Em   C G/B Am7 G
   We want to see Je - sus   lift - ed high

INTERLUDE:

G D   Em C

(REPEAT VERSE & CHORUS 1)

BRIDGE:

       D   Em
Step by step, we're moving forward
       D   Em
Little by little, taking ground
       D   Em
Ev'ry prayer a pow'rful weapon
       C   D
Strongholds come tumbling down
   and down and down and down

(REPEAT VERSE & CHORUS 1)

CHORUS 2:

G   D
   We're gonna see,   we're gonna see
Em   C G/B Am7 G
   We're gonna see Je - sus   lift - ed high
G   D
   We're gonna see,   we're gonna see
Em   C G/B Am7 G
   We're gonna see Je - sus   lift - ed high

OUTRO: *(Vocal ad lib.)*

G D   Em C

G D   Em C G/B Am7 G

WORTHY IS THE LAMB

DARLENE ZSCHECH

Key of **G Major, 4/4**

INTRO:

Em7   G   Em7   G

VERSE:

           C   **G/B**
Thank You for the cross, Lord

           C   **D** **G**
Thank You for the price You paid

       D/E   **Em7**   **D**   **C**
Bearing all my sin and shame, in love You came

   Am7   **G/B**   **D**
And gave amazing grace

G   **G/B**   **C**   **G/B**
Thank You for this love, Lord

         C   **D**   **G**
Thank You for the nail-pierced hands

       D/E   **Em7**   **D**   **C**
Washed me in Your cleansing flow, now all I know:

    Am7   **G/B**   **D**
Your forgiveness and embrace

CHORUS:

G   **D/F♯** **Am7** **G/B**   **C**
Worthy is the Lamb, seated on the throne

D   **D/C**   **G/B**   **C**   **Am7** **C/G** **D** **D/F♯**
Crown You now with many crowns, You reign victorious

G   **D/F♯** **Am7** **G/B**   **C**
High and lifted up, Jesus, Son of God

  D   **D/C** **G/B** **C**   **Dsus**
The Treasure of heaven crucified

     Am7 **G/B** **C**
Worthy is the Lamb

     Am7 **G/B** **Dsus**
Worthy is the Lamb

(REPEAT VERSE)

(REPEAT CHORUS 2X)

TAG:

         Am7 **G/B** **C**
Worthy is the Lamb

         Am7 **G/B** **Dsus**
Worthy is the Lamb

      G (hold)
Worthy is the Lamb

Worship Band Play-Along

The **Worship Band Play-Along** series is a flexible tool for worship leaders and bands. Each volume offers five separate, correlated book/CD packs: Guitar, Keyboard, Bass, Drumset, and Vocal. Bands can use the printed music and chord charts to play live together, and members can rehearse at home with the CD tracks. Worship leaders without a band can play/sing along with the CD for a fuller sound. The eight songs in each volume follow a similar theme for easy set selection, and the straightforward arrangements are perfect for bands of any level.

1. Holy Is the Lord

Includes: Agnus Dei • Be Unto Your Name • God of Wonders • Holy Is the Lord • It Is You • Open the Eyes of My Heart • We Fall Down • You Are Holy (Prince of Peace).

08740302	Vocal	$12.95
08740333	Keyboard	$12.95
08740334	Guitar	$12.95
08740335	Bass	$12.95
08740336	Drumset	$12.95

2. Here I Am to Worship

Includes: Come, Now Is the Time to Worship • Give Us Clean Hands • Hear Our Praises • Here I Am to Worship • I Give You My Heart • Let Everything That Has Breath • You Alone • You're Worthy of My Praise.

08740337	Vocal	$12.95
08740338	Keyboard	$12.95
08740409	Guitar	$12.95
08740441	Bass	$12.95
08740444	Drumset	$12.95

3. How Great Is Our God

Includes: Above All • Beautiful Savior (All My Days) • Days of Elijah • How Great Is Our God • Let My Words Be Few (I'll Stand in Awe of You) • No One Like You • Wonderful Maker • Yesterday, Today and Forever.

08740540	Vocal	$12.95
08740571	Keyboard	$12.95
08740572	Guitar	$12.95
08740608	Bass	$12.95
08740635	Drumset	$12.95

4. He Is Exalted

Includes: Beautiful One • God of All • He Is Exalted • In Christ Alone • Lord Most High • Lord, Reign in Me • We Want to See Jesus Lifted High • Worthy Is the Lamb.

08740646	Vocal	$12.99
08740651	Keyboard	$12.99
08740712	Guitar	$12.99
08740741	Bass	$12.99
08745665	Drumset	$12.99

5. Joy to the World

Angels We Have Heard on High • Away in a Manger • Hark! the Herald Angels Sing • Joy to the World • O Come, All Ye Faithful (Adeste Fideles) • O Come, O Come, Emmanuel • Silent Night • What Child Is This?.

08749919	Vocal	$12.99
08749920	Keyboard	$12.99
08749921	Guitar	$12.99
08749922	Bass	$12.99
08749923	Drumset	$12.99

FOR MORE INFORMATION, SEE YOUR LOCAL MUSIC DEALER, OR WRITE TO:

HAL•LEONARD®
CORPORATION
7777 W. BLUEMOUND RD. P.O. BOX 13819 MILWAUKEE, WI 53213

www.halleonard.com

Prices, contents, and availability subject to change without notice.

0709